EMMANUEL JOSEPH

The Unscripted Maestro, Turning Chaos into Charisma with Improvisational Genius

Copyright © 2025 by Emmanuel Joseph

All rights reserved. No part of this publication may be reproduced, stored or transmitted in any form or by any means, electronic, mechanical, photocopying, recording, scanning, or otherwise without written permission from the publisher. It is illegal to copy this book, post it to a website, or distribute it by any other means without permission.

First edition

This book was professionally typeset on Reedsy. Find out more at reedsy.com

Contents

1. Chapter 1 1
2. Chapter 1: The Birth of Genius 3
3. Chapter 2: The Art of Adaptation 4
4. Chapter 3: Embracing the Unknown 5
5. Chapter 4: The Power of Presence 6
6. Chapter 5: The Creative Mindset 7
7. Chapter 6: Turning Chaos into Charisma 8
8. Chapter 7: The Improvisational Leader 9
9. Chapter 8: Cultivating Resilience 10
10. Chapter 9: The Joy of Creation 11
11. Chapter 10: The Legacy of Improvisation 12
12. Chapter 11: The Future of Improvisation 13
13. Chapter 12: The Unscripted Maestro's Legacy 14
14. Chapter 13: The Mentorship Journey 15
15. Chapter 14: The Improvisational Innovator 16
16. Chapter 15: The Global Impact 17
17. Chapter 16: The Improvisational Philosopher 18
18. Chapter 17: The Celebration of Life 19

1

Chapter 1

Introduction to "The Unscripted Maestro: Turning Chaos into Charisma with Improvisational Genius"

Improvisation is the art of creating something remarkable out of the unexpected. It is the spontaneous, often unplanned creation that springs from the moment and flourishes without a script. In a world where predictability is often sought and uncertainty feared, improvisation stands as a testament to human ingenuity and adaptability. "The Unscripted Maestro: Turning Chaos into Charisma with Improvisational Genius" delves into the life and journey of Max, a master of improvisation who transforms chaos into brilliance with his exceptional talent.

Max's story is a beacon of inspiration for anyone who has ever felt overwhelmed by the unpredictable nature of life. From his humble beginnings in a small town to his rise as a renowned improvisational performer, Max's journey is a testament to the power of embracing the unknown. Through his experiences, we learn that improvisation is not just a skill confined to the stage but a way of life that can be applied to various aspects of our existence. Max's ability to navigate the unpredictable with grace and confidence teaches us valuable lessons about adaptability, creativity, and resilience.

The book explores the intricacies of Max's improvisational genius, shedding light on the principles and practices that define his approach. We delve into the art of adaptation, the importance of presence, and the joy of creation.

Through Max's eyes, we see how improvisation can turn the mundane into the extraordinary, transforming chaos into moments of pure charisma. Max's journey is a celebration of the human spirit's ability to thrive amidst uncertainty and find beauty in the unexpected.

Furthermore, "The Unscripted Maestro" examines the broader implications of improvisation beyond the arts. Max's story highlights how the principles of spontaneity and creativity can drive success in various fields, from business and innovation to education and leadership. His journey is a testament to the versatility of improvisational skills and their potential to inspire positive change in individuals and communities alike. Max's influence extends beyond the stage, demonstrating that the art of improvisation is a powerful tool for problem-solving and personal growth.

As we embark on this exploration of Max's life and legacy, we are invited to embrace the spirit of improvisation in our own lives. "The Unscripted Maestro" challenges us to view challenges as opportunities, to find joy in the present moment, and to turn our own lives into a masterpiece of improvisational genius. Max's story is a reminder that life itself is an unscripted journey, filled with endless possibilities and the potential for greatness. Through his experiences, we are inspired to navigate the chaos of life with creativity, resilience, and charisma.

Chapter 1: The Birth of Genius

In a small town, nestled between rolling hills and lush valleys, lived a boy named Max. From a young age, Max was known for his boundless energy and uncontainable curiosity. His parents often found him creating elaborate stories out of everyday events, turning mundane moments into grand adventures. Little did they know, this penchant for improvisation would become his greatest asset. Max's early years were marked by an insatiable desire to explore and understand the world around him. His mind was a canvas, constantly painting new ideas and scenarios. Despite the chaos that often surrounded him, Max thrived in the unpredictability, finding comfort in the unknown.

As Max grew older, his talent for improvisation became more apparent. In school, he excelled in drama and creative writing, effortlessly weaving narratives that captivated his classmates and teachers. His ability to think on his feet and adapt to any situation set him apart, earning him the nickname "The Unscripted Maestro." Max's journey was just beginning, and the world was about to witness the birth of a true genius.

Chapter 2: The Art of Adaptation

Max's teenage years were filled with challenges and opportunities that tested his improvisational skills. He joined the school's drama club, where he quickly became a standout performer. His ability to adapt to any role, no matter how complex or demanding, made him a favorite among directors and fellow actors. Max's performances were characterized by their spontaneity and authenticity, as he effortlessly brought characters to life.

Outside of the theater, Max's knack for improvisation extended to his social life. He became a master of navigating social situations, using his quick wit and charm to connect with people from all walks of life. Max's friends often marveled at his ability to turn awkward moments into memorable experiences, transforming chaos into charisma with ease.

Max's talent for adaptation wasn't limited to the stage or social interactions. He applied his improvisational genius to academics as well, tackling complex subjects with a creative approach that left his teachers in awe. Max's unique perspective allowed him to see solutions where others saw problems, and his relentless pursuit of knowledge fueled his growth as a true Renaissance individual.

4

Chapter 3: Embracing the Unknown

As Max entered adulthood, he faced a pivotal moment that would define his future. Unsatisfied with the conventional path laid out before him, Max decided to embrace the unknown and pursue his passion for improvisation. He left his hometown and ventured into the bustling city, where he sought out opportunities to hone his craft and share his gift with the world.

Max's journey was fraught with uncertainty, but his unwavering belief in his abilities kept him grounded. He joined an improv troupe, where he quickly rose to prominence as a dynamic and versatile performer. Max's performances were a testament to the power of spontaneity, as he fearlessly navigated the ever-changing landscape of live theater.

Embracing the unknown also meant facing setbacks and failures. Max encountered numerous challenges along the way, but each obstacle served as a stepping stone toward greater growth and understanding. He learned to view failure not as a defeat but as an opportunity to learn and evolve. Max's resilience and determination became the cornerstone of his improvisational genius.

Chapter 4: The Power of Presence

Max's journey of self-discovery led him to realize the importance of being present in the moment. In a world filled with distractions and noise, Max found solace in the practice of mindfulness. He discovered that true improvisation required a deep connection to the present, an awareness of the here and now that allowed him to respond authentically to whatever came his way.

Max's commitment to presence transformed his performances. Audiences were captivated by his ability to create magic on stage, drawing them into the story and making them feel like active participants. Max's charisma was undeniable, and his performances became a celebration of the human experience, filled with laughter, tears, and everything in between.

Offstage, Max's dedication to mindfulness extended to his personal life. He cultivated meaningful relationships, cherishing the moments he spent with loved ones and finding joy in the simple pleasures of life. Max's presence became a source of strength, allowing him to navigate the chaos of the world with grace and ease.

6

Chapter 5: The Creative Mindset

Max's journey taught him that improvisation was more than just a skill; it was a mindset. He realized that creativity thrived in an environment where flexibility and openness were embraced. Max began to view the world through a lens of possibility, seeing every challenge as an opportunity for innovation and growth.

To nurture his creative mindset, Max developed a series of practices that encouraged exploration and experimentation. He surrounded himself with diverse influences, seeking inspiration from art, music, literature, and nature. Max's curiosity knew no bounds, and he eagerly absorbed new ideas and perspectives.

Max also recognized the importance of collaboration in the creative process. He surrounded himself with like-minded individuals who shared his passion for improvisation and innovation. Together, they embarked on creative ventures that pushed the boundaries of what was possible, constantly challenging each other to think outside the box and embrace the unknown.

Chapter 6: Turning Chaos into Charisma

Max's journey culminated in a profound understanding of how to turn chaos into charisma. He realized that improvisation was not about avoiding chaos but rather embracing it and finding beauty within it. Max's ability to navigate uncertainty with confidence and poise became his defining trait, earning him a reputation as a true maestro of the unscripted.

Max's performances were a masterclass in charisma, as he effortlessly captivated audiences with his authenticity and charm. He used humor and vulnerability to create a connection with his audience, making them feel seen and heard. Max's charisma was a reflection of his deep understanding of the human experience, and his performances became a celebration of life's unpredictability.

Offstage, Max's charisma extended to his interactions with others. He used his improvisational skills to build meaningful relationships, turning strangers into friends and collaborators. Max's presence was magnetic, drawing people to him and inspiring them to embrace their own creative potential. His journey was a testament to the transformative power of improvisation.

Chapter 7: The Improvisational Leader

Max's success as a performer and creative mind led him to explore the role of leadership in the world of improvisation. He discovered that the principles of improvisation could be applied to leadership, creating a new paradigm for inspiring and guiding others. Max's journey into leadership began with a deep exploration of his own values and vision.

As an improvisational leader, Max emphasized the importance of collaboration and trust. He created an environment where team members felt empowered to take risks and think creatively. Max's leadership style was characterized by its flexibility and adaptability, as he encouraged his team to embrace the unknown and find innovative solutions to challenges.

Max's journey also taught him the value of empathy in leadership. He recognized that effective leaders needed to understand the needs and perspectives of their team members, and he used his improvisational skills to build strong connections and foster a sense of belonging. Max's leadership was a reflection of his belief in the power of improvisation to transform individuals and organizations.

9

Chapter 8: Cultivating Resilience

Max's journey was not without its share of setbacks and failures. He encountered numerous obstacles along the way, but each challenge served as a lesson in resilience. Max learned that the key to overcoming adversity was not to avoid it but to face it head-on with courage and determination.

Max's resilience was rooted in his improvisational mindset. He embraced uncertainty and viewed failure as an opportunity for growth. Max's ability to adapt and learn from his experiences became his greatest asset, allowing him to navigate the ups and downs of life with grace and confidence.

To cultivate resilience, Max developed a series of practices that strengthened his mental and emotional well-being. He prioritized self-care and mindfulness, creating a foundation of inner strength that allowed him to weather any storm. Max's journey was a testament to the power of resilience and the transformative impact of an improvisational mindset.

Chapter 9: The Joy of Creation

Max's journey was driven by a deep love for the creative process. He found joy in the act of creation, whether it was crafting a story, performing on stage, or collaborating with others. Max's passion for creativity was infectious, inspiring those around him to embrace their own creative potential.

Max's journey taught him that creativity was not limited to any one discipline or medium. He explored a wide range of artistic expressions, from painting and music to writing and dance. Max's curiosity and willingness to experiment allowed him to discover new forms of expression and push the boundaries of what was possible.

Max's joy in creation was also reflected in his commitment to lifelong learning. He continuously sought out new knowledge and skills, eager to expand his horizons and deepen his understanding of the world. Max's journey was a celebration of the creative spirit and the limitless possibilities that come from embracing one's passion.

11

Chapter 10: The Legacy of Improvisation

Max's journey of improvisation left a lasting impact on the world around him. His performances and creative endeavors inspired countless individuals to embrace their own creative potential and see the beauty in chaos. Max's legacy was a testament to the transformative power of improvisation and the profound impact it could have on individuals and communities.

Max's influence extended beyond the world of performance and into the realm of education. He became a passionate advocate for incorporating improvisation into the classroom, believing that it could help students develop essential life skills such as adaptability, creativity, and resilience. Max's efforts led to the creation of programs and workshops that empowered young minds to think outside the box and embrace their own improvisational genius.

Max's journey was a reminder that improvisation was not just a skill but a way of life. It encouraged individuals to embrace uncertainty, find joy in the present moment, and see challenges as opportunities for growth. Max's legacy was inspiring a new generation of improvisational geniuses who approached life with curiosity and creativity.

12

Chapter 11: The Future of Improvisation

As Max's influence continued to grow, he began to explore the future of improvisation in the digital age. He recognized the potential for technology to enhance and expand the possibilities of improvisation, creating new platforms for creative expression and collaboration. Max's journey into the world of digital improvisation was marked by a commitment to preserving the essence of spontaneity and authenticity.

Max collaborated with technologists and innovators to develop new tools and techniques that integrated improvisation into virtual and augmented reality experiences. These immersive environments allowed individuals to engage in real-time creative interactions, breaking down the barriers between performer and audience. Max's vision of the future was one where improvisation transcended physical boundaries, connecting people across the globe in a shared experience of creativity and joy.

Max also saw the potential for improvisation to play a role in addressing some of the world's most pressing challenges. He believed that the principles of adaptability, collaboration, and resilience could be applied to fields such as education, healthcare, and social innovation. Max's efforts to promote improvisation as a tool for positive change inspired a new wave of innovators and leaders who embraced the power of spontaneity and creativity.

13

Chapter 12: The Unscripted Maestro's Legacy

Max's journey came full circle as he reflected on the impact of his life's work. He realized that the true essence of improvisation lay in its ability to connect people and create meaningful experiences. Max's legacy was not just in the performances he gave or the accolades he received, but in the lives he touched and the communities he inspired.

Max's story became a source of inspiration for generations to come. His journey of turning chaos into charisma and embracing the unknown served as a guiding light for those who sought to live life with creativity and courage. Max's legacy was a testament to the transformative power of improvisation, a celebration of the human spirit's ability to thrive in the face of uncertainty.

In the end, Max's journey was a reminder that life itself is an improvisation, a series of unscripted moments that shape who we are and who we aspire to be. Max's story encouraged others to embrace the chaos, find joy in the present, and turn their own lives into a masterpiece of improvisational genius. The Unscripted Maestro's legacy lived on, inspiring a world where creativity and spontaneity were celebrated, and where the magic of improvisation could be found in every corner of life.

Chapter 13: The Mentorship Journey

As Max's reputation as an improvisational genius grew, he found himself in the role of a mentor. Aspiring performers and creative minds sought his guidance, eager to learn from the Unscripted Maestro. Max embraced this new chapter with enthusiasm, recognizing the opportunity to share his knowledge and inspire others to find their own path.

Max's mentorship was rooted in the principles of improvisation. He encouraged his mentees to embrace uncertainty and take risks, fostering an environment where experimentation and creativity thrived. Max's approach was hands-on, providing personalized feedback and support to help each individual unlock their unique potential.

Through his mentorship, Max witnessed the transformative power of improvisation in action. He saw his mentees grow in confidence and skill, turning chaos into charisma just as he had done. Max's journey as a mentor was a testament to the lasting impact of his teachings and the ripple effect of creativity.

15

Chapter 14: The Improvisational Innovator

Max's passion for improvisation extended beyond the arts, leading him to explore its applications in various fields. He became an advocate for improvisational techniques in business and innovation, believing that the principles of adaptability and creativity could drive success in any industry.

Max collaborated with entrepreneurs and business leaders to develop workshops and training programs that integrated improvisational practices into their operations. These programs encouraged teams to think outside the box, embrace change, and approach challenges with a creative mindset. Max's influence transformed organizations, fostering a culture of innovation and resilience.

Max's journey as an improvisational innovator showcased the versatility of his skills and the broad impact of his ideas. He demonstrated that improvisation was not just an artistic skill but a powerful tool for problem-solving and growth in all areas of life.

16

Chapter 15: The Global Impact

Max's journey took him beyond the confines of his own community, as he began to travel the world to share his message of improvisational genius. He conducted workshops, gave lectures, and performed in theaters across the globe, connecting with diverse audiences and cultures.

Max's global impact was profound. He inspired individuals from all walks of life to embrace improvisation and find beauty in chaos. His performances transcended language barriers, speaking to the universal human experience and the power of creativity. Max's journey became a bridge between cultures, fostering understanding and connection through the art of improvisation.

Through his travels, Max also learned from the people he met, gaining new perspectives and ideas that enriched his own practice. His journey was a testament to the power of cultural exchange and the transformative impact of improvisation on a global scale.

Chapter 16: The Improvisational Philosopher

As Max continued to explore the depths of improvisation, he delved into the philosophical aspects of his craft. He began to reflect on the deeper meaning of improvisation and its implications for the human experience. Max's journey as an improvisational philosopher led him to question the nature of creativity, spontaneity, and existence.

Max's philosophical musings were influenced by his encounters with thinkers and artists from around the world. He engaged in discussions and debates that challenged his understanding and expanded his horizons. Max's reflections on improvisation became a source of inspiration for his performances and teachings, adding a new layer of depth to his work.

Max's journey as an improvisational philosopher was a testament to his relentless curiosity and desire for understanding. He sought to uncover the essence of improvisation and its role in shaping the human experience, leaving a lasting legacy of insight and wisdom.

18

Chapter 17: The Celebration of Life

In the final chapter of Max's journey, he embraced the celebration of life through improvisation. He realized that every moment was an opportunity to create, connect, and find joy. Max's performances became a reflection of his appreciation for the beauty of the present, filled with spontaneity and authenticity.

Max's celebration of life extended beyond the stage. He cherished the moments he spent with loved ones, finding joy in the simple pleasures and the connections he had built along the way. Max's journey was a reminder that life itself was an improvisation, a series of unscripted moments that created a rich tapestry of experiences.

Max's story was a testament to the power of improvisation to transform lives and bring people together. His legacy lived on in the hearts and minds of those he had inspired, a celebration of creativity, resilience, and the unscripted beauty of life.

Book Description

"The Unscripted Maestro: Turning Chaos into Charisma with Improvisational Genius" is an inspiring tale that delves into the life of Max, a boy from a small town with an extraordinary talent for improvisation. This talent, seen early on in his ability to turn ordinary moments into grand adventures, grows into his defining skill as he navigates life's unpredictable paths. Max's journey, from his school days to becoming a renowned performer, showcases the transformative power of embracing the unknown.

The book highlights the art of adaptation and the importance of being present, as Max demonstrates how to turn chaos into moments of pure charisma. His story isn't just confined to the stage; it offers valuable lessons in creativity, resilience, and leadership, applicable to various aspects of life. Through Max's eyes, readers learn to view challenges as opportunities and to find beauty in the unexpected.

Max's journey is a celebration of the human spirit's ability to thrive in uncertainty. His experiences teach us that improvisation is not just a skill but a way of life that can drive success in diverse fields, from business to education. The book inspires readers to embrace spontaneity, think creatively, and connect meaningfully with others.

"The Unscripted Maestro" also explores Max's role as a mentor and innovator, emphasizing the broader impact of improvisational skills. Max's story becomes a bridge between cultures, fostering understanding and connection through the art of improvisation. It is a testament to the power of creativity to inspire positive change and transform lives.

Ultimately, the book is a reminder that life itself is an unscripted journey filled with endless possibilities. Max's story encourages readers to navigate the chaos of life with creativity, resilience, and charisma, turning their own lives into a masterpiece of improvisational genius.

www.ingramcontent.com/pod-product-compliance
Lightning Source LLC
LaVergne TN
LVHW020509080526
838202LV00057B/6255